W9-CLW-442

101 Things to Do Before You Turn 40

101 Things to Do Before You Turn 40

Kristin McCracken

BERKLEY BOOKS, NEW YORK

THE BERKLEY PUBLISHING GROUP
Published by the Penguin Group
Penguin Group (USA) Inc.
375 Hudson Street, New York, New York 10014, USA

Penguin Group (Canada), 10 Alcorn Avenue, Toronto, Ontario M4V 3B2, Canada
(a division of Pearson Penguin Canada Inc.)
Penguin Books Ltd., 80 Strand, London WC2R 0RL, England
Penguin Group Ireland, 25 St. Stephen's Green, Dublin 2, Ireland (a division of Penguin
Books Ltd.)
Penguin Group (Australia), 250 Camberwell Road, Camberwell, Victoria 3124, Australia
(a division of Pearson Australia Group Pty. Ltd.)
Penguin Books India Pvt. Ltd., 11 Community Centre, Panchsheel Park, New Delhi—110 017,
India
Penguin Group (NZ), cnr Airborne and Rosedale Roads, Albany, Auckland 1310, New
Zealand (a division of Pearson New Zealand Ltd.)
Penguin Books (South Africa) (Pty.) Ltd., 24 Sturdee Avenue, Rosebank, Johannesburg
2196, South Africa

Penguin Books Ltd., Registered Offices: 80 Strand, London WC2R 0RL, England

Copyright © 2005 by The Berkley Publishing Group
Cover design by Rita Frangie.
Book design by Tiffany Estreicher

PRINTING HISTORY
Berkley trade paperback edition / September 2005

Library of Congress Cataloging-in-Publication Data

McCracken, Kristin.
    101 things to do before you turn 40 / Kristin McCracken.
        p.   cm.
    ISBN 0-425-20236-4
    1. Conduct of life—Miscellanea. I. Title: One hundred one things to do before you turn
forty. II. Title: One hundred and one things to do before you turn forty. III. Title.

    BJ1595.M42 2005
    646.7—dc22   2004062788

PRINTED IN THE UNITED STATES OF AMERICA

10   9   8   7   6   5   4   3   2   1

I am indebted to the web of friends whose contributions gave life to this list; to my Sunday afternoon editors who, when plied with wine, told me exactly what they thought; and to Jenny and Aimee for getting the ball rolling.

Quit your book club.

Yeah, I said it. During the '90s, Oprah convinced us that we all needed to start reading more, and to follow up by sharing the experience. She was right, and she got us all reading weepy chick lit, but now even she seems a little tired of the concept. As a former English major, I admit I would be extremely well-read if I read everything I was assigned. But I didn't. Childishly— but instinctively—I resented *having* to read the book, so I resisted. Or I skimmed. In adulthood, we have all gotten ourselves into the same boat. Face it: Book clubs annoy everyone. You're rarely interested in the book, and you fall into one of two camps: 1) You're the one who always reads the whole thing (sometimes cramming the night before) and no one else does (so who are you sharing the experience with?), or 2) You feel guilty about not finishing, after lugging that albatross of a hardcover around with you for a month. Stop doing this to yourself. Read the books you like, at your own pace, and if you don't like something, put it down and move on. If you do like it, pass it along to a smart, literate friend, and then have lunch to discuss it when she's finished. And for Pete's sake, don't rush her.

Bridge the baby chasm.

It's a fact: Motherhood can come between girlfriends. When your best friend has a baby and you don't, your relationship changes. I call it the "baby chasm"—it's always deep, but it doesn't have to be wide. There are some women who totally transform into mommies, full of hearts and flowers, never to be heard from again. With those friends, look back, smile, wish them well, and move on. Maybe someday you'll see them on the other side. With the friends who really matter, though, you can work through it. After the initial talk about Diaper Genies and burpcloths (about which you can firmly tell her you do not care), ask her the hard questions, and let her tell you the answers. She's going to need her confidant: about her sore nipples, her incompetent husband, the other mothers she finds as annoying as you do, and how odd and terrifying it feels to be responsible for another life. Find a way to keep her grounded. Without being condescending, encourage her to take a girls' night out, give her great books to read, or take her to a spa. Be there for her, and be the hippest auntie there is.

Admit to everything.

We all play games. It's tempting to be coy, to never admit when we're wrong, to keep a certain sense of mystery. But a candid woman is a refreshing thing. When you make a mistake (or hurt someone's feelings), at work or in your personal life, own up; don't let it simmer quietly, eating away at you from the inside out. If the situation warrants it, come clean, apologize, and make an effort to right the wrong. (Love does *not* mean never having to say you're sorry.) You'll feel better, and your admission will often defuse the situation, because no one can equitably fault you for being human. Own the decisions you think are right, and defend them in the face of disagreement. Explain your position articulately, and with straightforward certitude. Own your actions, too, while you're at it. So you smoked a little dope, or had a relapse with a poisonous ex-boyfriend, or you taught yourself how to do a raunchy pole dance. 'Fess up and move on.

Throw an Oscar party.

Did the guys ban you from their Super Bowl party for looking at fashion magazines during the plays and demanding silence during the commercials? In response, institute an annual get-together of your own that's just as sacred. Throw an Oscar party a month later. Welcome guests with your own red carpet, hoot and holler at the real arrivals on TV, place bets on the winners, and give out decadent goodie bags upon departure. If overhyped movie stars aren't your thing, make your annual bash a New Year's Day open house, with hangover remedies galore. Or host a "Breakfast at Wimbledon" pajama party, complete with strawberries and cream. Or get together with some friends and throw a Halloween costume ball; change the theme each year to keep it fresh. After a couple of years, you are guaranteed "tradition" status, and you will become legendary.

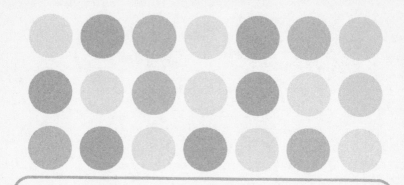

Make out with
the best man.

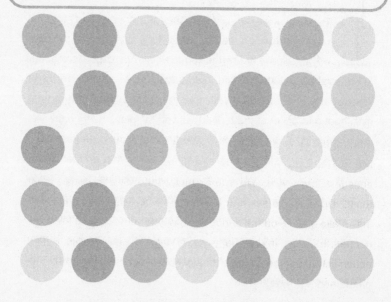

I love weddings, and I'm usually thrilled for my tying-the-knot friends. But if there's one thing I dread, it's that calligraphied "and guest," blinking like neon when I'm not dating someone. So I decided to let my friends do the work for me. Why tie myself down to a date I scrounge up last-minute, when I don't really like him enough to go out with him in the real world? Weddings don't always have to be about the bride and groom. Think of them as great places to meet someone your friends have already vetted. Yeah, the best man (or the single guy the bride knowingly seated you next to) may live in Timbuktu, and he may not be your ideal mate. But if he's guestless, too, why not get to know him, especially if he gives a great toast? Once you've set your sights, don't be a bridesmaid-in-waiting—make a move on the dance floor. Maybe you'll make a love connection, but even if what happens in Vegas stays in Vegas, a little action somehow seems more magical when accompanied by champagne and a tuxedo.

Eat the worm.

My friend Jenny swears that tequila is the best thing to drink when you're feeling down. But don't forget the worm. It's said to hold magical, mystical powers of happiness beyond belief. It might be squishy, but it's known to have ethereal effects, and unlike absinthe, it's legal in this country. (Well, as far as I know, anyway.) Does it scare you? All the better. Sushi probably did at first, too. Wherever you can, look for ways to broaden your horizons. You might draw the line at sweetbreads or brains, but then again, they might become your favorite delicacies. So the next time you're offered something that makes you wrinkle your nose, stifle the instinct to say no. Nod, smile, chew, and swallow.

Build a nest egg.

By now, you probably have a growing 401(k) or 403(b); if not, get your assets in gear. Once you've got that covered, consider other potential investments that will fund your kick-ass retirement. Real estate is a risk-averse, solid choice—if you think you can't afford to buy, think again. Mortgage rates vary, there are programs for first-time buyers, and your parents might be delighted to loan you the down payment. If you already own a home, think about saving for a vacation property in an up-and-coming development area; if you get in on the ground floor, you'll watch your seed money multiply. Don't be afraid to accept professional help—a good financial advisor can help you delineate long-term and short-term goals, and sometimes fees are waived once you invest. As soon as you know what you're looking for, read the financial pages; start small and buy some stocks to watch. No matter what route you choose, take control of your money. You've worked hard for it. Now make it work for you.

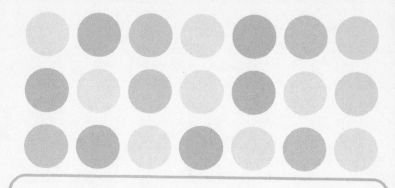

Take your parents
out to dinner.

Old habits are the hardest to break, especially when they involve family dynamics. Nothing's harder than not reverting to your childhood role the minute Mommy is in the room. But the next time your folks are in town (or you're back home), reverse roles and treat your parents to a special night out. Give them some warning, and let them know your intentions. They might resist at first, but they'll probably be delighted and swelled with pride in the long run. (Just don't remind your dad that you earn more than he does.) At dinner, ask your parents to tell you about how they met, or how they got engaged. Be interested in their lives. Consider this one more step toward breaking the patterns of youth. As the role reversal evolves over the next decade (or two or three), you'll want your parents to learn to value your advice as much as you value theirs.

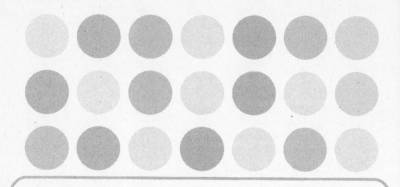

Date a twenty-five-year-old, one last time.

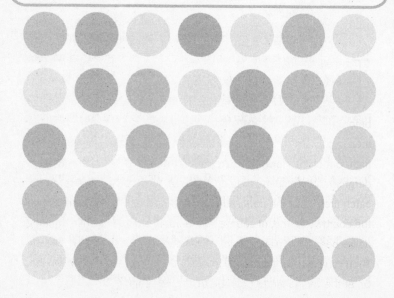

It's almost time for us single women to start looking for financially stable men who will make appropriate husbands, fathers, and partners in life. These men will help us age gracefully, but before that happens, find a boytoy and have one last fling. Younger men are totally in vogue, and they can be quite an accessory for a night out on the town. If you'd prefer, though, to keep your fling underground, then spend time doing things thirtysomethings rarely do: catch fireflies in the park, build a sand castle, or play Skee-Ball on the boardwalk. And, of course, make out in a dive bar while drinking dollar beers and playing pool. Go ahead, get it out of your system. Then you just might be ready to settle down and live a grown-up life. Or, at the very least, to upgrade to a thirty-year-old.

Put a lid on it.

"Great minds talk about ideas; mediocre minds talk about events; small minds talk about people." If this anonymous quote is true, then quite often, my mind has walked dangerously close to the tiny side. But I'm working on it. Gossiping about others (even if we think we're well meaning) can be snarky fun, but it can easily get us into hot water. (Once you accidentally hit "reply" when you meant to hit "forward," you'll find out how impossible it is to retract an e-mail that's been sent out into the ether.) Once you get the reputation of being a Nosey Nellie, people will stop confiding in you, for fear of general broadcast. Then you'll get no scoop, ever.

Karaoke.

Take a couple of bottles of sake, add some cheesy pop classics, and mix with a few overconfident exhibitionists who aren't afraid of a microphone. You may be shaking your head, but I firmly believe that everyone has an inner diva just clamoring for attention; she should be coaxed out, nurtured, and worshipped. The next time you are hemming and hawing about what to do for kicks, shed your inhibitions once and for all and find a tacky local bar with a karaoke night. Promise yourself you won't back out; take this opportunity to be the center of attention. (If you *must,* ask your friends to sing backup the first time, but sing solo the next round.) Pick a song to interpret—a '70s groove classic, some Aretha soul, a standard or show tune, an '80s power ballad—and make it your own. (In Japan, everyone has a signature song.) Don't go for the obvious, consider song length carefully (a song with a never-ending chorus wears out its welcome), and shoot for high crowd participation to get the audience on your side.

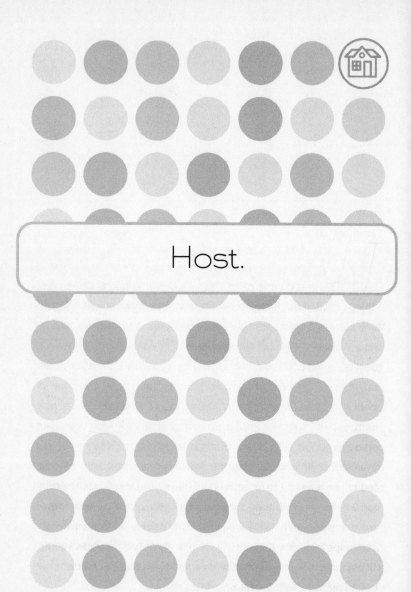

Host.

When I was younger, my guests were lucky if they got a fresh pillowcase, let alone a gourmet breakfast. Well, I still don't have a spare bedroom, but I have learned a thing or two about how to treat visitors. When entertaining friends, think of their comfort first: Always make sure there's plenty of wine and snacks in the house (first things first!) and that each sleepover guest gets clean sheets, two towels, and a washcloth. Aside from that, it's the little things that make all the difference. By saving hotel freebies, you can easily put together little Marthalike gift bags—shampoo, conditioner, soap, razor, toothbrush—and have a shower cap on hand. Let them know that whatever's yours is theirs; in the days before cell phones, my uncle Dan would be offended if anyone tried to use a calling card rather than dialing direct. (This is also the man who warms your towels in the dryer before you take a shower—now that's service!) Aside from comfort, double as a concierge—have maps available for your city, and suggest fun activities you all will enjoy. Don't worry about overdoing it—eventually, no matter how welcoming you are, they *will* want to go home.

Scuba dive.

I am a big fan of snorkeling, which is easy to do once you get past the initial panic of not breathing through your nose. Sand irritates the hell out of me, but I LOVE being in the ocean, so fish-gazing gives me something to do while my friends are basting themselves on the shore. Despite scary shark movies, scuba diving seems like a natural next step. A few years ago, my sister learned how to dive, and since then, this hobby has taken her all over the world. She saw six-foot clams(!) during a live-aboard trip off the Great Barrier Reef, spent a week diving off a private island in Belize, and did a night dive in Fiji, which was as illuminating as the glow-in-the-dark fish. Certification classes aren't hard to find—usually you practice in a reservoir or some such. Don't think about *Jaws,* and don't hold your breath.

Document your life.

Over the years, you may have kept sporadic (or meticulous) journals of your thoughts and doings, and you've taken pictures on all your travels. But what kind of order are they in? Can you name all the people in your childhood snapshots, let alone your class portraits? Before it's too late, enhance your cranial memory bank. Make a timeline of your own life, with photos and captions. Create a visual family tree, filling in the blanks with help from your elders. Ask your parents questions about childhood homes that are a bit fuzzy in your mind, and write down the stories that are repeated at family gatherings; it's important not to let that kind of oral history get away from you. Reminiscing helps you build layers into your memories, and it keeps things fresh in your mind. Go online and trace your roots back to the old country. Find out where you came from, and resolve to keep track of where you're headed.

Stop the tchotchkes.

A few years ago, my parents downsized from their five-bedroom house in the suburbs to a two-bedroom, deluxe apartment in the city skyline. To do this, they obviously ridded themselves of all extraneous tchotchkes, picture frames, and dishes. At the same time, my mother issued an edict against any gift that was not consumable, unless specifically requested. We all took this to heart, and I've since totally jumped on her bandwagon. When I used to have a birthday deadline, I tried to put thought into gifts, but I also sometimes went to my favorite tchotchke supplier and mindlessly picked out something adorable and useless. Now, instead of *things*, we give each other *experiences*: massages and pedicures, cooking classes, gift certificates for movies and baseball games, museum memberships, glider rides. When you consider the recipient, these gifts can be as thoughtful and personalized as the old approach, sometimes even more so.

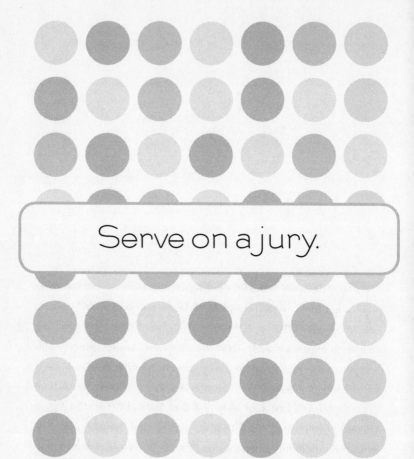

Serve on a jury.

I must have an honest face. Each of the three times I've been called to jury duty, I was selected to serve. One time, I was the foreperson on a double murder trial; I was twenty-one years old (beginner's luck, I guess). This intense lesson in civil responsibility also gave me an eye-opening glimpse into humanity. Juries are a cross section of society, and the whole process illuminates the trust and responsibility each of us is given, by the mere fact that we are citizens of voting age. It's a disgrace that so many people take pride in shirking their duty when they could instead be a part of an amazing, complicated human microcosm, faced with determining an outcome that can have such an impact on a fellow soul. (The guy we convicted will be in jail until at least 2041; he deserves to be there, but it was a tough decision.) Of course there's no way to guarantee that you will be selected next time you're called, but at least don't actively avoid the possibility.

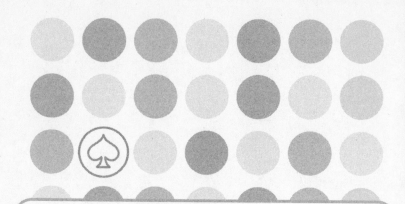

Play poker.

Kenny Rogers was on to something. Playing cards is a great metaphor for life (with all the holding and the folding and the walking away). If you haven't learned (or don't understand) these ancient lessons yet, pick up a deck of cards and a copy of *Hoyle's Rules of Games* and shuffle up. Rule #1: Nothing is a bigger "tell" than having to ask in the middle of a hand what beats what. A flush beats a straight; four of a kind beats a full house; and a straight flush beats everything else. Rule #2: You don't always have to have great cards to win; attitude is everything. Bluffing is a priceless talent; if you can control your emotions and your facial tics, you'll be in good shape. On the flip side, reading people's faces with dexterity gives you an edge, in cards and in life. Poker is hot right now—you can watch the intense World Series of Poker on ESPN, or see your favorite B-list celebrities duke it out for charity on Bravo's *Celebrity Poker Showdown*—so it shouldn't be hard to find people who play. If you can't get into a regular game, or you aren't ready to face off with experienced players, invite some buddies over for a practice game, pass out the candy cigars, and ante up. There'll be time enough for talking when the dealing's done.

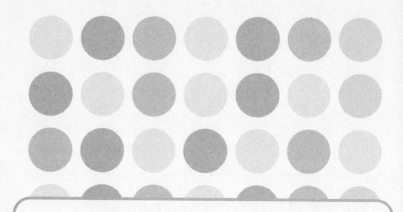

Musically upgrade.

Do you still have boxes full of cassette tapes in the far reaches of your closet? How about milk crates of record albums you haven't listened to since 1986? Face facts: Albums and cassettes have melted into oblivion, at least figuratively. Take stock of your musical holdings, and cultivate your own harmonious identity. A grown woman should have a sophisticated and diverse musical library, reflecting the breadth and depth of her urbane tastes. Make a list of your must-have classic recordings and get the remastered versions on CD. If there are mixed tapes you can't bear to part with, go online and buy the individual songs you want, giving your sentimental favorites a technological lease on life. Don't let the new stuff get away from you—keep your ears open and ask about (and follow up on) things you hear and like. Don't be afraid to broaden your horizons: a little hip-hop never hurt anyone. Neither did a good aria, for that matter.

Yell at someone.

This is so much easier said than done, especially if Miss Manners (in the form of your mother) lives inside your head. But sometimes expressing your anger is called for, and it can feel oh-so-good to get things off your chest. First of all, make sure the recipient of your wrath deserves it, and is not just doing his or her job. Second, give the intended yellee a chance to explain and/or apologize; full-throat venom should be reserved for people who will neither admit their mistakes nor take responsibility seriously. Once you are sure your outburst has met these criteria, let it fly. Teach that cheating boyfriend that honesty really is the best policy, or tell that contractor exactly where he can stick his monkey wrench.

Remove it.

If you are fair haired and not at all hirsute, then you can just turn the page. If, however, you have ever obsessed about removing your unwanted hair (chin, lip, bikini, the works), then let's talk. You work hard to look your best, and you probably attacked those few stray whiskers (okay, a veritable mustache, in some cases) when they first began to rain on your gorgeousness parade. But now you're tired of the upkeep. First of all, electrolysis is painful, and not as permanent as you'd like it to be after all that you've endured. Waxing is a major hassle to keep up, and ingrown hairs can be a bitch. Bleaching only masks the problem, because the hair is still there, and it grows thicker as we get older. And face it, you can't buy Nair with a straight face; it's just too '70s (and that *song*—who, exactly, wears short shorts?). Plucking? Please. Shaving? It works in a pinch, but stubble sucks. But don't give up, because luckily, there is a newfangled option: lasers. They are not just for Princess Leia anymore. Yes, it's still a bit pricey, and you need to commit to several cycles in order to reach the full effect (and not everyone is a good candidate). But I know you'd invest gladly if they promised hair removal so permanent you could throw away all those products you got suckered into on the late-night infomercials.

Lose the snooze.

I s "Just eight more minutes" your morning mantra? Do you know the minimum amount of time (to the second) you need for your morning routine without being radically late to the office? Do you cut corners, skipping breakfast and putting your makeup on in the rearview mirror? This is what we call "the snooze factor," and it causes us unnecessary havoc. Instead of starting the day off with such chaos, get up the minute your alarm goes off, the first time. This will give you a chance to adjust to the day at a civilized, the-house-is-not-burning-down pace. Have coffee at home while browsing the morning paper or check your e-mail at leisure. Feed the cat. Review your schedule for the day. See what Katie and Matt are up to. Allow yourself to stretch and maybe even throw in a few sit-ups before you hop in the shower. You don't have to become a morning person if it's not your nature, but maybe you'll learn to appreciate the quiet time before the hectic pace of the day kicks into high gear.

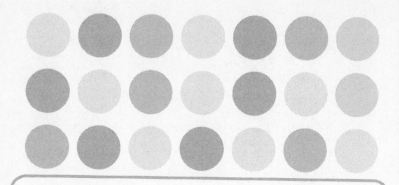

Pierce something
other than your ear.

Now that you've accepted your body for what it is—including your belly, your gut, your tummy—decide on some ornamentation. Face it: tattoos are too permanent, and will only expand over time. Instead, why not do what comes naturally? Find something sparkly and fasten it to your body. A belly-button ring is not permanent, and no one has to see it unless you choose to show it off (baby tees are a whole other kettle of fish; you're on your own there), but *you'll* know it's there, and you'll feel sexier for it. My friend Cecelia got hers at age thirty-eight, and she is my hero.

Strain your brain.

Don't ignore your mental agility. Evidence suggests that keeping your brain active and challenged can alleviate normal memory loss and even postpone the onset of more serious afflictions such as Alzheimer's disease. To engage your mind, take up a daily crossword puzzle, join a bridge club (it's not just for grandmas anymore), or play Scrabble against the computer. A strategic game of chess can be an excellent alternative to a night with the boob tube. Put away the trashy beach paperback and pick up a more highbrow read than you're used to (and look up any words you don't know). You don't have to join Mensa, but up your game a bit. You're smarter than you think. Most of us work out regularly to keep our bodies in good working order and to stave off the aging process. That's all well and good, but as you get older, do you really want your heart ticking away if your mind is in la-la land?

Rent the classics.

Forget *Citizen Kane* and everything you learned in film history class. For me, a movie's value is not measured in theme, leitmotif, or foreshadowing. Instead, it's calculated by the amount of dash, class, sass, and moxie it contains. Old movies can be very instructional. Watch how Kate Hepburn wins Cary Grant over with her feistiness. (But don't forget that Scarlett O'Hara went too far.) Study how Barbara Stanwyck drops her handkerchief for Henry Fonda to pick up gallantly. Marvel at the way Bette Davis transforms from wallflower to femme fatale. Admire Lauren Bacall's ballsiness as she teaches Humphrey Bogart how to whistle. These prefeminists used their womanly wiles wisely, and their men didn't stand a chance. After you've absorbed in the lessons they have to teach, go out and do it yourself. Cinch your waist, order a dry martini, doll yourself up in false eyelashes, and bat them wisely. Turn heads. Blush. Swoon a little.

Pay off credit card debt.

Maybe it started in college, with those tempting offers encouraging you to build a credit rating. Perhaps you justified your increasing debt with the excuse, "I need more miles!" throughout your twenties. Now you may not be as bad off as some of those women you see on Jerry Springer, who keep buying and buying while their debt level hits the stratosphere. Still, if you are carrying any balances from month to month, you are pretty much mitigating any and all savings from that drastically-on-sale dress you thought you couldn't afford *not* to buy. You may need to tighten your purse strings for a while, but think how good it will feel to head into your forties debt-free. Once you're out of that hole, you'll have more money to spend, without all the guilt. Save the credit card for emergencies. You'll be able to afford your own plane ticket—paid for in cash.

Think outside the box.

It started out innocently enough: a few errant grays started popping up around your hairline, and you pulled them out without panicking. Soon enough, though, they multiplied, as they do, and you knew you had to make a move. You watched TV commercials intently, and took Heather Locklear's advice (since when is that a good idea?), agreeing you *were* worth it, after all. After splurging on a $7.99 box of haircolor, you were calmed into thinking this would work. But what happened? The blond highlights you were promised came out decidedly orange, the grays came back anyway, and the bloom was off the rose. Isn't your hair worth more than that? It's time to give in, if you haven't already. Make an appointment, 'fess up to creating the rug that is your overprocessed, self-dyed mop, and beg for help. You know Sarah Jessica Parker does not *really* do it at home.

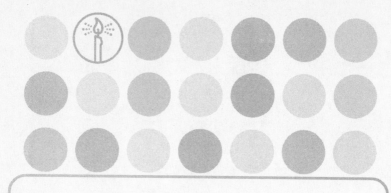

Do something
romantically cheesy.

My sardonic nature, unfortunately, often prevents me from being as gushy as I have the potential to be. But once in a while, I allow myself to stop the eye-rolling and act on my romantic impulses. When this happens, I want to hold hands and make out in the movies, swim under a waterfall, ride a bicycle built for two, and go on a hot air balloon ride at sunset. If you feel this urge, go with it. Plant love notes in his briefcase, tucked alongside candy hearts. Give him a mortifying nickname (but not in front of his friends—have *some* dignity). Buy dozens of roses and blaze a petal path to the bedroom. Take a bubble bath together. (No matter what, though, draw the line at baby talk; it's *not* attractive on adults.) Eventually, this schmoopiness will fade, and you'll go back to being your cynical, lovable self. In the meantime, get a room.

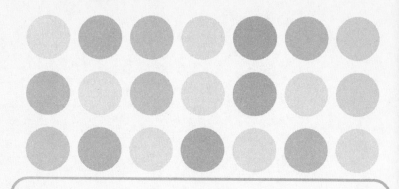

Drop $50 on a bottle of wine.

By this point in your life, long gone are the days of Riunite and Boone's Farm. So are the parties where guzzling straight from the keg was encouraged. But while your tastes have improved, have your spending habits? Since you're not drinking as much as you used to, you have more of a chance to *appreciate* the glass or two you enjoy with dinner. While I honestly don't believe that a $2,000 bottle of wine is exponentially better than one that costs $200 (though I would welcome a taste test), I am certainly convinced that spending a bit more on the low end of the spectrum makes a significant difference. If you like wine, start shopping around. Invite your friends over for a better-wine-tasting party (B.Y.O.-$20–50B.; you'll supply the cheese) and really try to learn something. Taste, savor, and compare. Once you find a few things you like, make a note and keep your cellar well stocked. (Buying cases is a cost-efficient way to save.) Leave the boxed wine in the dust.

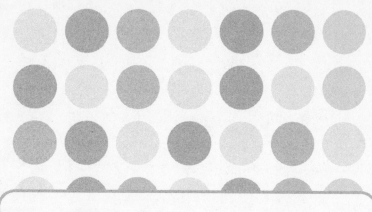
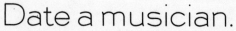

Date a musician.

My very first crush was on David Cassidy. I ordered Partridge Family records from TV commercials, I had a pillowcase with his picture on it, and I kissed the album cover picture of him gazing thoughtfully at his horse. I soon moved on to his brother Shaun, and eventually to a succession of replacements over the years. (No matter how cheesy he's become, I still love Rod Stewart. Sue me.) Old habits die hard. Before it's too late, find a musician and make him yours, at least for a little while. Go to his gigs, stare down his groupies (real or imagined), and believe that every song he writes is about you. Stroke his ego and be the supportive muse. Get him to sing for you in bed . . . naked. Before you turn into Yoko, though, realize that unless you are willing to live in smoky dive bars and yawn on the way to work in the morning (someone has to be the breadwinner), gaze thoughtfully into his eyes and explain that you're taking *your* show on the road. He can turn his pain into inspiration for his next ballad.

Drive cross-country.

Our fascination with foreign travel sometimes causes us to discount the fun to be had right under our noses. No country has the diversity of ours. So . . . Count the rainbows over Niagara Falls. Walk the boardwalk in Atlantic City. Bicycle across the Golden Gate Bridge. Cross the Badlands. See a Broadway show. Get a mud bath in Napa Valley and then drink wine in the vineyards. Stand on the Four Corners. Pose in front of Mount Rushmore. Sing "Suspicious Minds" outside of Graceland. Whitewater raft down the Colorado River. Ride up the Gateway Arch in St. Louis. Storm the Alamo. Go to Disney World. Hike the Appalachian Trail. Eat a peach in Atlanta. Find the Statue of Liberty from atop the Empire State Building. Have a cocktail on Bourbon Street. Gamble at a $100 table in Vegas. Protest outside the White House. Visit the pandas at the San Diego Zoo. Marvel at Chicago from the top of the Sears Tower. Water-ski on Lake Winnipesaukee. Hike the Grand Tetons. Check in on Old Faithful in Yellowstone. Watch the sun set over the Grand Canyon. Not necessarily in this order, of course.

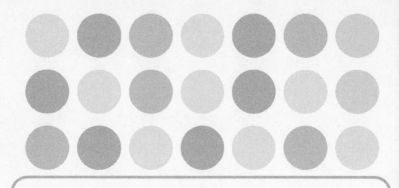

Control the future
of your face.

Washing nightly with soap (or falling into bed with your makeup still on) may have worked for the first few decades of your life. But now you've noticed a certain dryness to your face, and your pores have begun to fissure unattractively. Sure, you may take the pessimistic view and tell yourself Botox is always an option. But you're not "of a certain age" yet, so why not take the preventative route while you still can? Wash your face with a rich cleanser that's right for your skin type every night, without exception. Moisturize, moisturize, moisturize—the more good stuff you slather on your skin, the better. While you're at it, remove your eye makeup with cold cream to keep crow's feet at bay. And the cardinal rule, which is (of course) often the hardest to keep: Whether it's in your makeup or your moisturizer, use SPF protection whenever you're in the sun. Don't get conned into $50 eye creams. Instead, trawl the drugstore aisles, read the labels, and experiment. Do you think your problems would be better handled by a professional? Make a date with a dermatologist or get a facial. Ask them what's right for you, and stick with it. Find the right formula for you while you can still make a difference.

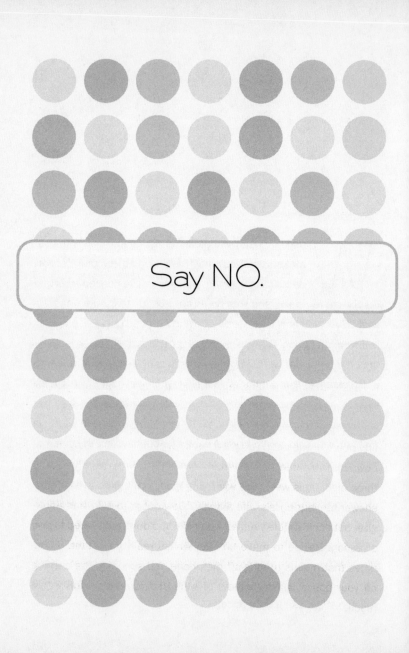

Say NO.

There's certainly something to be said for responsibility, and for being accommodating, but sometimes we have difficulty putting our feet down when we really need to. There are only 168 hours in a week, and you have to sleep once in a while. Plan for downtime, and don't overschedule your life. You work fifty hours a week and you have family obligations? It's okay to turn down that volunteer request from the ASPCA. You're already booked three nights this week and you didn't really want to go to that baby shower for your boss's wife anyway? Bow out gracefully and apologize, but don't saddle yourself with guilt. You don't even need to give a reason. Decide to make time for what's really important. Sometimes that means turning off the phone and spending the evening on your couch, glass (bottle?) of wine and remote control within reach.

Ride a Harley.

Imagine all that horsepower between your legs, the wind in your hair, and the danger coursing through your veins . . . If you've never been on a motorcycle, you've never really taken a walk on the wild side. Find a Hell's Angel (or a decent substitute) and ask him to take you for a ride. Wear a helmet—and full body leather, if you've got it—and hold on tight. If you find that too terrifying, and you really just can't pull the trigger, ride a mechanical bull instead. There are no highways involved, and not even any horns to avoid. Have a couple of longnecks to steady your nerves, don your best Lady Stetson, and take the reins. You're an urban cowgirl who can handle eight seconds of anything with a honky-tonk crowd cheering you on. And if you're lucky, you'll get to roll in the hay when you're finished.

Accentuate the positive.

If you're in a traffic jam, and there's absolutely nothing you can do about it, do you instinctively start fuming anyway, even though there's no one to blame? If a friend asks in passing how you are, do you immediately groan and start listing off your maladies and irritations? Oh, that sounds fun, for you *and* her. Listen to yourself: the kvetching, the whining, the woe-is-me tirade. Just stop. You may indeed be tired because you got up early, but you don't have to complain about it. It's the classic half-full/half-empty diametric. Do you see yourself as a victim or as an agent for positive change? Negativity is exhausting, pointless, and it drives people away. Instead, think about something terrific that's in the works (there's always something) and talk about that instead. If nothing good is happening in your life, then whose fault is that? Take the initiative and change something for the better. Do you want to be happy today? Think about it; you have a choice.

Say yes to bubbles.

There are few enough reasons to celebrate, so why not take advantage of each one that comes along? Make it your personal policy to accept champagne whenever it's offered, and also to proactively find reasons to celebrate. Instead of waiting for good news to arrive, or saving your celebratory energy up for that far-off milestone, create your own reason to rejoice. Popping a cork adds a festive bolt to any occasion, and it always brings out the giddiness in a crowd. It can charge up a routine Sunday brunch, evoke New Year's Eves gone by (a holiday always more appealing in retrospect, if you ask me), or promise a future full of caviar dreams. No home is complete without at least four delicate champagne flutes. Keep them sparkling and at the ready; with bubbly on ice, you'll always be prepared. Occasions to celebrate don't age like fine wine, and they aren't finite in number. Gather your friends, pop the cork, and toast your communal good fortune.

Redistribute the wealth.

You can always tell which one of your friends has worked as a waitress, because she is always the most generous tipper in restaurants. She knows that what goes around, comes around. If you've never worked in a service industry—retail, hotel management, a gas station—you may not have been on the receiving end of an unreasonable customer's ire. Thank your lucky stars, appreciate the help, and resolve to never be that kind of blowhard. But think about those who help you out, and don't forget them around the holidays; know how much to give your hairdresser, your super, your cleaning lady. On the more anonymous side, did you know that you are supposed to leave a modest tip for hotel maids, either every day or upon your departure? You probably did, but somehow, this practice completely eluded my awareness until my mid-twenties. I would like to take this opportunity, in print, to apologize to the twenty-five years' worth of hard workers who picked up my towels and changed my sheets.

Unsubscribe.

How much mail do you get every day? How many magazines arrive each month? Each week? Be honest. Magazines are life-suckers of the highest order, especially trashy ones. I mean, how many *Cosmo* quizzes have you taken over the years? Do you ever learn anything about you or your partner? Their biggest threat is their tendency to travel in packs. Don't they just pile up, unread, staring at you—blank-eyed, airbrushed and anorexic, guilt-inducing—until you throw them out, still unread? Pare down your subscriptions to the one (or two—okay) that you can't live without. If it's *People*, fine, I won't judge—I, of all people, understand the need for brain candy. (Call me a snob, but I live for my *New Yorker*, and I read it cover to cover.) But cancel everything else. Instead, make magazines a special treat: buy them in airports, on the beach, or after you've finished a long novel. Or go early to your next doctor's appointment and catch up. Just keep them out of the house.

Confront bullies,
racists, and
homophobes.

Over time, smart people change their minds as they absorb more information about the world. Unfortunately, wisdom doesn't *always* come with age; stubbornness, biases, and ingrained prejudice can color our worldview and allow us to stagnate. For this reason, we should help each other keep our minds open and fertile. Try to listen to different viewpoints and reconcile them with your own; sometimes you'll be successful, but some things you can't let slide, and I don't think you should. Try not to be obnoxious about it, but if an acquaintance makes derogatory and hateful statements rooted in stereotypes—even if not directed at you—it's your duty to register your offense. (My friend Susan still smarts about the time she didn't stand up to her friend who made a racist comment; she worries that her silence was assumed to be a tacit concurrence, which is probably the case.) How far you want to go, and whom you decide to confront, is a personal choice. Even if you can't change the world, you can still try to change a mind.

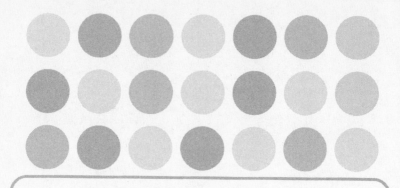

Supply your
own power.

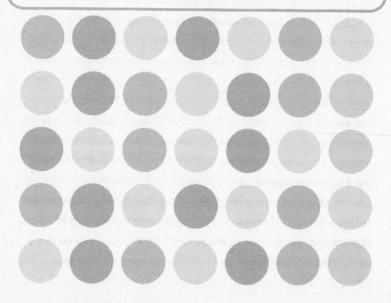

These days, thirtysomethings are fairly computer-savvy. But is your VCR still blinking "12:00—12:00—12:00"? (Should you still even be using a VCR?) Are your digital photos stuck inside your camera indefinitely? Are you still using a Walkman? With non-rechargeable batteries? A girl has to keep up with the times, or else she runs the risk of sounding like the spinster aunt bemoaning the death of her rotary phone. But you are not an old dog; you *can* learn new tricks. Don't be afraid to tackle challenges by defying the stereotype. The next time the tech guys come into your cube, pay attention. Learn how to do minor troubleshooting. Understand the difference between Wi-Fi and Firewire. Hook up your own DVD player; you can follow instructions, and I know you can tell red from yellow from white. Hell, if you need to, ask a kid for help. They expect adults to be clueless, and they know how to do everything. But pay attention when you do, so you can do it yourself next time.

Sculpt yourself.

Now that you've settled into your thirties, you have a little time left to get your body into the shape you want it to stay in for the long haul. Take a good look at yourself. What can you live with? Recognize that there are some things you can't do anything about (the knobbiness of your knees, the inevitable shifts of gravity), at least not without major surgery. But if there are major things you want to—and can—change (weight loss, muscle tone), do it now; it's much easier to maintain than to overhaul as we get older. When it's all said and done, you need to come to terms with some of what makes you YOU. Once you figure that out, a dress size is just a number; it's not a reflection of your worth or your lovability. If you can't accept the way you are, you're facing constant misery and wishing your life away. No one is perfect. No one. Even Charlize Theron has flaws (somewhere). Learn to accentuate your good points and to camouflage the not-so-good. Love yourself for who and what you are, and others will, too. But accept everything. And worry about world peace instead.

Teach a class.

Think of all the things you are good at, and pick one to share with others. You don't have to find an adjunct instructor position, although the extra cash wouldn't hurt, so if you can, knock yourself out. Otherwise, start simple: Invite your friends over and bring out your basket of knitting needles, or volunteer to hold a session at work on the latest computer skill you've mastered. If you're feeling a little more adventurous and/or confident, find a local community center and teach English as a Second Language or basic grammar skills. You could plant a community garden and invite local kids in for a Saturday morning master class on growing things. Or contact the local Learning Annex and propose a one-night lecture on something you know a lot about, whether it's the cultural history of Guatemala or navigating the new tax codes.

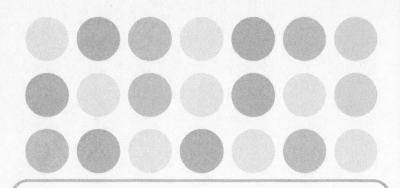

Have a kid if
you want one.

In generations past, women didn't think twice—only true renegades didn't get married and have kids in their twenties. As we progress into this new millennium, however, the thirties decade is now a period fraught with life decisions, not the least of which are *The Baby Questions:* Do you want one? If not, will you regret it (and will your mother forgive you)? If so, how long should you—could you—wait before trying? How many will you have? Do you need a partner to have one? Will you work or stay at home? Of course, I can't give you answers; these are personal questions each woman has to consider for herself. But unfortunately, this issue has a relative shelf life: The chances of having a healthy baby start to decrease drastically after thirty-five (excluding adoption), as does your energy level. If you're having trouble deciding, get the skinny from friends with kids. Research the price of a college education. Spend the weekend with your nieces and nephews. If you decide you want a kid around permanently, don't worry if you don't have all the trappings. Get cracking and procreate; the rest will fall into place.

Go to Paris.

Paris lives up to all its hype—it's a magical place in any season, big and old and beautiful and full of hidden treasures. On a misty day, leave your lipstick kiss on Oscar Wilde's tombstone in Père Lachaise (Jim Morrison's grave is underwhelming). Ride to the top of the Eiffel Tower (it only *sounds* cheesy) and feel like the queen of all you survey. Kiss someone on a bridge over the Seine (pick any bridge, or anyone). Get drunk on art (don't miss the Big Three paintings at the Louvre, but search out obscure museums, too), and support the local painters in Montmartre. Meditate inside Notre Dame, and light a candle at Sacre Coeur. Longingly admire the haute couture, even if it's out of your price range. Inhale the flowers in the Luxembourg Gardens, or any garden, really. Every day, eat crepes and croissants for breakfast, and have *steak frites* with really good wine for dinner. Wear your walking shoes and carry a good map. Don't be afraid to live the clichés; Paris invites them, defies them, and gives them new life.

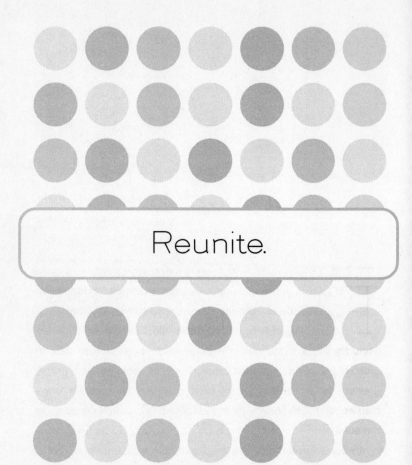

Reunite.

Friends are mostly associated with different periods in one's life: childhood, college, post-college, and those who have spanned several of the above. Going the furthest back, my posse of high school buddies is now spread out nation-wide, but we ignore distance and keep in touch; e-mail and cell phones are heaven-sent. Beyond that, though, we also unfailingly plan weekend reunions every two years or so, in someone's house in the suburbs or in a hotel in a centrally located city. (When Ann recently pulled up stakes and hightailed it to Hawaii, we had an Aloha weekend in New York City.) Pick a group of friends who are important to you. Plan regular weekends where you get together—just the girls—and watch the time apart fall away. Stay up late and make new memories. Some people are surprised by twenty-year friendships, but I'm not. It's not easy to stay connected, but then again, the important things never are.

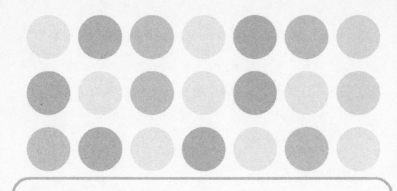

Be your own
Schneider.

Every woman should have a fully stocked toolbox in her arsenal—look for tools designed especially for women—and she should know what every gizmo is used for. (If you don't have the tools you need, give your dad a birthday list. He will be *thrilled* to buy you a drill; any excuse to go to Home Depot . . .) If you are not exactly the fixer-upper type, ask a friend who *is* over for an afternoon and take a crash course in Handywoman 101. Practice on little things around the house that annoy you: the wobbly doorknob, the drippy faucet, the loose cabinet hinge. Once you've mastered the indoor devices, head out to the garage for Car Maintenance 202. Cell phones have saved many a modern damsel in distress on the side of the highway, but what do you do when you're out of range on the back roads? You don't need to know how to reconstruct a taken-apart engine, but you'll feel empowered the first time you distinguish a radiator leak from a spark plug malfunction. Of course, in all do-it-yourself endeavors, there is a fine line between handy and overconfident: know when you're in over your head, and keep that list of emergency numbers (the electrician, the plumber, the mechanic) within easy reach.

Give a really great toast.

Does public speaking make you weak in the knees? Tackle your fear head-on and practice, because I guarantee that sometime soon you will have to make the perfect toast, and it *will* be videotaped. Take the advice of a three-time maid of honor: Be fully prepared to give a toast that will be remembered for years. There are two cardinal rules for good speech-giving: 1) Be completely comfortable with your topic, inside and out; and 2) Know your audience. Give yourself plenty of lead time, brainstorm about what you really want to say about the guest of honor, and then do some sifting—if a thread naturally emerges, use it as a theme and build on it. Practice plenty, adding inflections and pausing for laugh lines. As for audiences, most people assume that family and friends are a piece of cake, but they can actually make you more nervous than strangers. If this happens, remember that these people love you, or at least they love the toastee. Find a good buddy in the audience and speak directly to her. Smile a lot, make eye contact, and let a few tears slip through; this is my recipe for a heartfelt and unforgettable toast. Just don't ever watch the videotape.

Buy a piece of real art.

By now you've gotten rid of the Doisneau posters from college, but have you actually spent money on art? Art is something to be collected and enjoyed, and it can be found in all kinds of places (but *not* at the mall; Thomas Kinkade is not for discerning palates). Support friends who are genuine artists, and make a point of bringing back a hangable souvenir from each of your travel destinations. If you take care of these pieces, they can be tangible, sometimes sentimental, evocations of times gone by. Recognize, however, that these are not necessarily *subjectively* valuable. When you're ready to branch out, go searching for a piece with a real frame and a hefty price tag. Aside from shopping in expensive galleries in art-laden hot spots, you can also find undiscovered gems at local art shows and auctions. College studio programs have shows for their graduates; if you select wisely, you might be investing in the next Jackson Pollock.

Take a stand.

Democracy is a good thing, where every individual has a voice that should be valued and heard, and not just on Election Day (though that's an ideal place to start). Unfortunately, few women take full advantage of this right; instead, they let others decide what happens in this country—socially, economically, politically—and then complain about the outcomes. To rectify this, we need to be well informed, giving our voices weight and credence. Start by reading the newspaper every day, and not just the Style section; it's your responsibility to learn about the issues, and to decide where you stand. What gets you fired up? Once you figure it out, and have evidence to back up your stance, do something. Go to a political march. Write a letter to the editor. Attend a school board meeting. Run for office. At the very least, remember that a bunch of heroines fought for your right to vote, which they won fewer than one hundred years ago. (We've come a long way, baby.) To honor them, and out of respect for yourself, vote in *every single election* held in your district. And know what you're voting for.

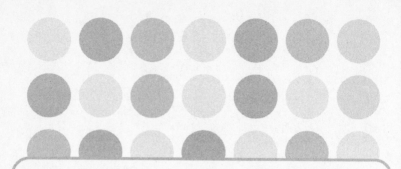

Master a mass-transit
system, but know
how to hail a taxi.

My mother has lived all over the world (albeit mostly in suburbs), so when she came to visit me in the city, I didn't think twice about leaving her on her own for the day while I went to work. I left her detailed instructions about how to take the subway uptown to see a particular exhibit, confident of her ability to navigate her way. Imagine my surprise, then, when I came home to find her decidedly ecstatic about her journey on the subway by herself. It never occurred to me that she would be nervous about taking the train, but she was. She confessed that while I was giving her directions, she had already decided to take a taxi and keep it to herself. After I left, though, she gave herself a pep talk: She could do it, without my father or me, and she would prove it. That was ten years ago, and now she and my father live in a big city of their own—Chicago. My mother walks everywhere, rides the bus, and sometimes even takes the "El," though she knows when it's okay to take a taxi. Don't wait until you're in your fifties; keep your wallet tucked away and leave the car at home.

Cut someone loose.

After thirtysomething years, you've accumulated a lot of friends. You've amassed even more acquaintances; some of them are annoying and useless, and some of them are just life-suckers. How do you get rid of the human equivalent of a piece of driftwood? The same way you break up with men you are finished with. First, you can try the easy way out (as if she were a dreary blind date): Don't return her calls, and politely but firmly decline when she suggests plans. If she just won't take the hint, you've got to decide if the next move is to bluntly cut her loose. If she's somehow wronged you, tell her she hurt you, and that you don't want that toxicity in your life. If that's not the case, fudge a little and explain that you are concentrating on work for the next few months, or that you're imposing a drastic budget and need to cut back on going out for the time being, or that you want to concentrate on the new man in your life. It's not her, it's you—and you need to figure out what relationships are most important to you, and focus your energy on how to make them stronger.

Vibrate.

In this age of *Sex and the City* and beyond, women are much more forthcoming in admitting and embracing their sexual needs and preferences. We all have Samantha—and HBO—to thank for that. There is another movement afoot that encourages women in their thirties to get to know their bodies and become more than just a passive partner in the bedroom. On any given night, groups of women are gathered in suburban living rooms, discovering gadgets and creams that will spice up their marital (and nonmarital) relationships. Sex toys are the new Tupperware. There are "Slumber Parties," "Pleasure Parties," more parties than you ever thought possible—where women are learning to take advantage of the rumored peak of their sexual satisfaction (thirty-five and counting, apparently). Find the one nearest you or host one yourself. Whether you have a sexual partner or not, invest in a quality multispeed vibrator, and learn how to use it expertly. As one of my friends—who wishes to remain anonymous—explains, "I have two kids and a full-time job. I don't have time to mess around!" If you do have more time on your hands, though, introduce your toy into your relationship. Teaching someone else to use it on you doesn't have to be embarrassing; experimenting together just might double the fun.

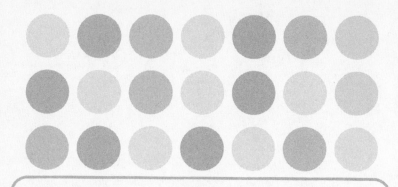

Enact a two-drink maximum.

Being tipsy as a twentysomething was sometimes charming, or at least you thought so; being drunk never was at all. And in our late twenties, my friends and I started to notice that we didn't bounce back like we used to; hangovers tended to invade our heads more intensely, and after fewer and fewer drinks. I haven't totally shunned excess—given the right time or place, and the right designated driver—because certain occasions definitely call for overindulgence, but as a rule, two drinks should certainly be enough. Instead of inadvertently getting smashed, concentrate on the people you're with, and savor the experience. You don't have to be a teetotaler: a glass of wine (or two) with dinner is lovely, and/or a snifter of cognac for dessert might mellow you out. Any more than that, though, and you can start to feel out of control, and your words tend to follow; it's nearly impossible to take your foot out of your mouth the next morning. Remember—a six-pack of beer is not a serving size, and bottles of wine can be safely recorked for another day.

Play an instrument.

Do you remember dreading the forced-upon-you piano lessons as much as I did as a kid? I still hear the metronome in my sleep once in a while, but I am so grateful that I know how to read music (however rustily) and can still plink out a meager *Für Elise* if I have to. I have my forward-thinking parents to thank for that, and for the cringes I get when I think about what a brat I must have been at times. Recently, I've become a bit wistful for my long-ago musical past, and I've decided to take up where I left off. I bought a book of hippie-chick sheet music (Joni Mitchell, anyone?) and worked through some of the rust on my joints. At the encouragement of a then-boyfriend, I bought a banjo and developed a new appreciation for twang, even though it took some time to train my fingers. Don't assume you're past your musical prime; Madonna learned to play the guitar at forty-two. So pick an instrument (either familiar to you or brand-spanking-new), take some lessons, and make some joyful noise.

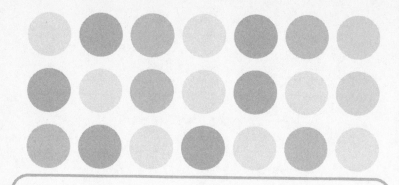

Make a new friend
each year.

Remember that old chestnut about making new friends but keeping the old? Well, the Girl Scouts got two things right (the other being Thin Mints), even if your green sash of patches is buried in your mother's attic. Remember how exciting the first day of school used to be? You got to see friends you hadn't seen all summer, but there was also that delicious possibility that you would meet a new friend in third period. As adults, we don't get to do that as often anymore; we sometimes feel too strapped for time even to see our old buddies as much as we'd like. Still, it's important to bring new faces into our circles. New people challenge us in ways that can be fresh and exciting; as we get to know someone for the first time, we also rediscover things we didn't know about ourselves. So make an effort to turn an acquaintance into a friend. If there's someone you work with who walks that fine line, invite her to lunch and talk about things that aren't work-related. Maybe there's a friend of a friend you'd like to get to know independently; if so, build on something you have in common—make plans to see a foreign film or take your dogs to the park.

Smell good.

We've all been the elevator-riding victims of an overzealous scent-applier. I knew a woman once who seemingly rolled around in lighter fluid before a night out on the town. But a tastefully selected (and sparingly applied), sweet-smelling nectar can make you irresistible. Some women are known for their scents—I know you can name one of these friends (and smell her in your mind) without even blinking—but I'm much less of a monogamist. Snowglobes and stamps don't smell good; I collect perfumes instead. Feminine or musky, flowery or fruity, cheap or expensive; I know what I like when I smell it. One word of advice: Never, ever, test scents in a duty-free shop before a flight. Somewhere out there is a planeful of passengers to London who are still cursing me to this day.

Dump the Gap.

I recognize that the Gap is known for its back-to-the-basics style and shop-without-thinking ubiquity. But at some point, start supplementing your everyday wardrobe with real clothes that are neither disposable nor replaceable on any corner, and that actually say something distinctive about you and your style. Once you start thinking about each purchase and valuing quality over quantity, you will no longer find things in the back of your closet with the tags still on that you don't even remember buying. Instead, you'll be excited every time you put together an outfit. And don't worry about things going out of style—if you avoid buying things with trendy logos prominently displayed, your clothes will be with you for the long haul. Buy pieces that flatter you, and you'll build a wardrobe to be envied. For a real treat, splurge on a classic black-tie dress, and pick a designer you've heard of. Think of how great it will feel each and every time you can say "I'm wearing Chanel tonight." Just make sure you know how to pronounce it.

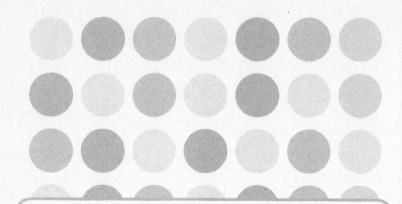

Boycott February 14.

Who the hell was Saint Valentine, and where, exactly, did Cupid's arrow shoot him? Don't always give Hallmark the satisfaction of your blind acceptance. Just once, skip the pressure of finding the perfect lovey-dovey (price-hiked!) restaurant when your relationship is doing just fine on its own, thank you. (You can always go out the next night, or buy each other flowers on "just because" occasions.) Instead, spend one Valentine's Day with your best girlfriends (no husbands or boyfriends allowed) and have your own lovefest. Make a gooey chocolate fondue (use the good stuff) and pair it with copious amounts of Veuve Clicquot (champagne named for a widow who ran her own vineyard). Then, if you feel like it, go dancing, or have a slumber party. Trust me, any left-out menfolk will feel only relief, and the single among you will appreciate the girl-power reprieve from the seasonal fake-holiday–induced depression.

Take a sabbatical.

At this point in your life, you've likely been working full time for quite a few years. If you are among the lucky few, you work for a university that rewards a lifelong approach to learning. Sabbaticals are an opportunity to leave your real life behind for six months or a year and learn something new, to restore your creative reserve, and to rejuvenate your zest for life. If you are not this fortunate, you might need to create your own break from the world. While (if) you're not tied down, think about subletting your apartment and traveling from Finland to Antarctica to Oaxaca to Mumbai, like my friend Elizabeth did. Or, like my friend Katie, you might choose to put your things in storage, move to Rome for a while, and reevaluate your life; she came back refreshed and ready to tackle the world. Maybe a good long summer vacation at the shore is all you need. Sometimes you need to be absent from your real life in order to fully enjoy it.

Go fishing.

We live in a world that does not offer us many opportunities to commune fully with nature, so when we can, we should take full advantage. One of the purest manifestations of the Darwinian principle is asserting our dominance over other species, and luckily our brainpower affords us the luxury of avoiding messy, hand-to-hand combat. Instead, get up before the sun one morning (or pick a lazy afternoon), drive to the nearest lake or pier, claim your grassy knoll or wooden plank, and bait your hook. (If you've never done this before, you'll need someone to provide the hook. And the bait. And the instructive demo.) Whether it's catch-and-release or you cook up your quarry for dinner doesn't really matter (although nothing tastes like fresh fish, the well-earned fruit of your labor). Get lost in the process of it all, and don't wear a watch.

Fill up your jewelry box.

Jewelry is a funny thing. Women are encouraged by the world (and convinced by tradition) to sentimentalize stones and rocks and metal, and most of us comply. Generally, I find this commendable, but sometimes I wonder why, when jewelry is so personal, we let someone else pick out our baubles. If your jewelry collection is mostly made up of costume fun you've picked up here and there, with a few good pieces-of-glory from your grandmother or the like thrown in for good measure, take charge and add to your collection of heirlooms. Each year or two, shop around and decide on one piece you love. It doesn't cost to look at Cartier or Bulgari, but sometimes you can find great deals at auctions, estate sales, and antique jewelry stores. When you find the piece you want, crave it a little bit, savor the anticipation, and then splurge. You might start with a string of pearls, a fabulous watch, or a really special ring. Work your way up to substantial diamond earrings, and take good care of them. Someday, your granddaughter will be glad you did.

Kiss the frogs.

As we all know from watching TV (and just breathing in general), dating can be a situation fraught with land mines for single women in their thirties. As people around you get married, panic sets in, and you develop beer goggles without the beer. It may be imperceptible at first, but soon you find yourself looking at the fifty-year-old plumber's butt crack with more than a little forgiveness. (Hey, he's employed!) Stop right there. You are a clever, rocking, funny knockout woman with a lot to offer the right guy. (And I'm not just saying that.) So get out there and start kissing frogs. As my friend Barb insists, "You only have to meet *one* right guy, and there are so many out there." He's not going to just show up at your front door—be proactive about your search. You never know where you might meet that very special frog: it may the guy on match.com, or your aunt's podiatrist she's been hinting about, or that blind date your colleague insists you go on. You may even have to take a deep breath and ask out that guy you've had a crush on for a month. Regardless, you have to be in it to win it. And don't settle for someone who doesn't knock your socks off. If he's not right for you, make a clean getaway and allow yourself to move on with no strings attached. Hold out for the prince, because you're worth the wait.

Play matchmaker.

Once you've found the love of your life, start working on your friends. Whenever you meet someone new and interesting, check for a ring and ask the right questions—subtly, of course. But really *think* about which of your friends this person might be good for—don't make the classic mistake of thinking that just because two people are single and straight (or Catholic, or lawyers . . .), they'll have a lot in common. If you're even more ambitious, throw a party for single friends only, with the caveat that every woman must bring a platonic male friend they are not interested in, and vice versa. (This will keep the ratio even.) Be warned—many people will steer you away from this dangerous path, and they have a point: You could be asking for trouble, or getting yourself into a messy situation if things don't work out. So plan ahead: To avoid blame down the road, make your no-strings-attached speech up-front and loudly. Then forge ahead. How happy will you be when you make a real love connection? You can give a toast at their wedding, and bask in their lifelong awe and devotion. The truth is, everyone needs a benevolent busybody once in a while, so why shouldn't it be you?

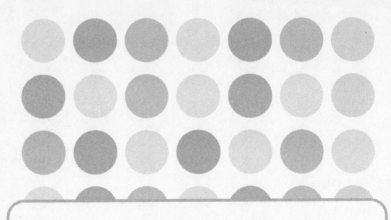

Be a boss.

Most of us have had many bosses over the years, and from each we've learned something about management, positive or negative. Chances are, you now have people who report to you or at least look to you for guidance. Decide what kind of boss you want to be, and act accordingly. The best one I ever had believed in the power of vacations for rejuvenation and refueling; she also mentored each member of her staff, ensuring we learned new things under her watch, and making us all more marketable when looking for future positions. Women still get a bad rap in the office world; make sure you do your part to counter the notion of "female-boss-as-ballbuster," but don't be a doormat, either. Treating your employees as colleagues will earn you their respect, as will meaning it when you say you want to keep the lines of communication open. Depending on your situation, you might ask for feedback on your own performance—perhaps even anonymously—and take the suggestions to heart.

Purge.

When I was a kid, my family moved every three years or so. Aside from being heartbreakingly painful (saying good-bye to friends, adjusting to new schools), this was a good thing. Not only did I learn how to connect with people right away, and get to see the country and the world, but I also had to evaluate my possessions on a regular basis. Now, I've been in the same apartment for eight years (a record for me), and I recently started to feel like my apartment was closing in on me. It wasn't that my living quarters were too small (though my most frequently recurring dream is that I have a whole other room I never knew about, fully furnished!), but instead, I had too much stuff. Since I hadn't moved in so long, I had not been forced to throw anything out, and it was taking its toll. My organization-guru sister came for the weekend, and she was ruthless. We pretended I was moving (the true test was whether I would pay movers to haul something or not; if not, out it went), and cleaned the place out, keeping only the things I really loved. All of a sudden my apartment is livable again, and I feel like I have a new lease on life. It has inspired me to think before I buy, and to not bring more crap into my life. I'm not quite a minimalist yet, but I am getting there.

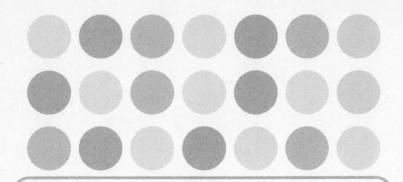

Break your
own record.

When I was in my twenties, no one I knew had run a marathon. Now, however, it's become (almost, not quite) commonplace among my thirtysomething friends, and I'm impressed. Not only do they cite the cheering spectators as inspiration, but they also highlight the adrenaline rush that comes from achieving something they didn't think they were capable of. Pushing yourself physically is a way to keep yourself young and limber, and it can boost you into peak condition, physically and mentally. My cousin Jackie joined her local crew team, and her arms have never looked better. Find something you like, and test your endurance while you're still young enough to accomplish greatness. Do you swim? Take it to the next level and join a competitive team, or backstroke across a lake. Do you hike on the weekends? Vow to climb a really big rock or Mount Kilimanjaro. If you're not feeling so *Into Thin Air,* leave the stationary bike behind and cycle around Utah like my friend Nancy. Forget the StairMaster; race up the Empire State Building instead. Be competitive with yourself, and don't let anyone tell you you're too old to set records.

Quit smoking.

All right, you've said you're doing it a million times. What happened? This time, say it like you mean it and get the job done. Take control: go cold turkey, get hypnosis, wear the patch, chew the gum—whatever works. The health benefits are so fundamental you don't even need to hear them again. Also, who wants to stand around outside in the cold like a leper, just for a dismal puff? If those aren't reward enough, create incentives for yourself: use the money you're saving to pay for luxuries you thought you couldn't afford. Schedule regular massages, or make a fancy dinner reservation a month in advance. If you fall off the wagon, deny yourself the reward. You can do this. Your heart and lungs (and teeth! and clothes!) will thank you.

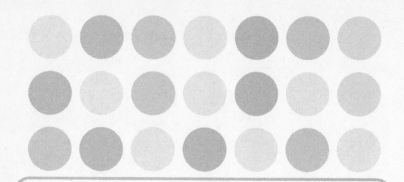

Sign each book
you read.

For your own little piece of immortality, you don't need to write a book. Instead, be an active participant in the writer/reader relationship. Sign the back page of every book you read, and date it accordingly. If you're like me and have a mild case of Obsessive-Compulsive Disorder, it will help you remember when you finished it (when you just have to know, for no reason at all). And when you pass it along—notice I said *when,* not *if:* I believe every book should have more than one home in its lifetime, or else it hasn't fulfilled its purpose—everyone who reads the book later will know you read it. Start with this one. Maybe others will follow your lead. Maybe we'll start a craze. The librarians will hate me.

Ask a friend for help.

As you approach forty, you might believe you've earned your moniker of Independent Woman, and that you are wholly self-sufficient. At the same time, you might have become the Rock among your friends, the one everyone comes to for support, guidance, and a dry shoulder. Deep down, you know your friends would do anything for you, but you haven't asked in so long that the needy muscle feels rusty. This can be dangerous—you start to suppress your needs, and you forget that life is not an isolated journey. Nip this in the bud. The next time you are feeling down, anxious, or confused (or even just lonely), call up your best buddy. Tell her what you're feeling, and ask her for what you need— a funny movie, a boost of confidence, a hot cappuccino, or just a friendly face. She'll be glad she can return the favor this time, and the connection will do you good. Just don't ask her to help you move.

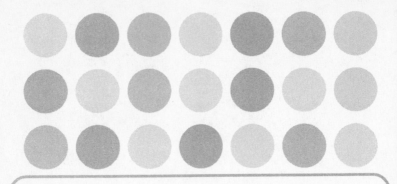

Drive a car that costs
more than $50,000.

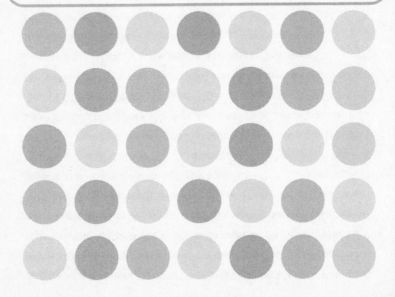

So you still drive that Toyota, circa 1996. It works, and it gets great gas mileage, even if you have to roll up your window manually. I don't care about that. Yet just because you can't afford to *own* a hot rod, it doesn't mean you don't deserve the good life once in a while. Go to the BMW dealership and ask to test drive one overnight. (And don't mess around with an automatic; to really feel the power at your fingertips, you need a stick shift.) After you've taken it for a spin on the open road, park it in front of your house and take a picture. Or, the next time you're out of town, rent a Mercedes convertible, put the pedal to the metal, and head for the beach, singing along to Blondie at top volume. After your trip, go home and start a new-car savings fund—symbolic or not—in a shoebox decorated with photos of you in the driver's seat.

Show gratitude.

One of the mantras that my mother drilled into my head was, "Always write a thank-you note." (Another one, "Always wear a slip," has stayed with me as well, though it's not as universal.) My sister and I had to finish our Christmas batch of thank-you's before New Year's or we were in big trouble. As usual, she was right. Thank-you notes let people know you have manners, and that you appreciate even the smallest gesture. (Not to be greedy, but they also increase your chances of getting a repeat gift next year.) Send thank-you notes not just for presents, but also to host/esses of events (weddings, dinner parties), to a salesperson for a job well done, and as a follow-up after job interviews (you never know what might tip the balance between two good candidates). And don't forget to thank your family; they shouldn't be taken for granted. Recently, my friends and I added a new twist to this issue: At a shower for a friend who had a very full plate, and who is very conscientious about etiquette, we gave her a final gift card that read, "No thank-you notes necessary." I'm sure it was hard for her to accept, but I bet she was grateful.

Expose the wizard.

We all love to be entertained, and we usually appreciate the second (or third) degree of separation a TV or silver screen provides. But at least once, try to get behind the scenes for a glimpse of how it all comes together. Next time you are in Los Angeles or New York, attend a late-night talk show taping and inhale the corniness. Or, if you have any tangential relation (cousin of a friend of a brother-in-law) working on a movie set, see if you can wrangle a visit. You'd be amazed at how *un*glamorous it all is, and how much waiting around it entails. If just being a spectator is too passive for you, try out for a game show. (I don't recommend reality shows unless you have a masochistic streak, and don't mind being the laughingstock of the water cooler.) Aim high: My friend Kristine and I (and her dad) confidently tried out for *Jeopardy!* one time (well, twice, if we're being completely honest), and were sufficiently knocked down a few pegs when the BEST score among us was three out of ten. (You needed seven just to move on to the next round.) Someday we'll try again. In the meantime, at least I've seen Letterman.

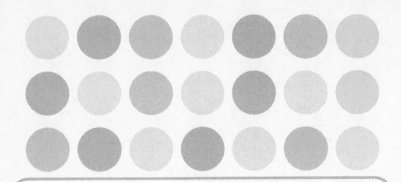

Take a
mental-health day.

As the oldest child, I always had this "must follow the rules and please everyone" complex. The one exception was that I would fake being sick and try to stay home from school. And I liked school. I don't know what that's all about. I think it was the delicious prospect of a day home alone with my books, my records, and yes, the TV. It didn't work very often—my mother is one shrewd fraud-detector. As an adult, most of us are afforded this underused luxury: sick days. What a brilliant concept! The only problem is that when you're really sick, they aren't much fun. I propose that once a year (I'm not advocating taking advantage), you call in sick and don't tell anyone. The office won't fall apart without you for a day. But don't clutter your day with lunch with friends downtown, or by doing your laundry. Have an alone day, at home (stay in bed with a cheesy novel) or out in the world. I would take myself to the multiplex and make my own triple feature, subsisting on popcorn and a gallon of Diet Coke. Just don't tell my boss.

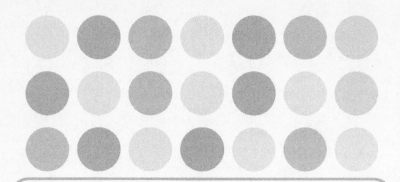

Discover your
superpower.

Maybe you can tie a knot in a cherry stem with your tongue, or get out the tangliest of tangles in jewelry chains. Maybe you're the one who always shows up with the made-from-scratch birthday cakes. Maybe you do impressions, or you can raise a lone eyebrow and wiggle your ears at the same time. No matter what it is, though, you've got a special talent that no one knows about . . . or that some people know about . . . or that you're famous for. Of course, it's more fun when your superpower is something you can bring out with a flourish at your next party (gravity-defying body parts don't qualify)—like card tricks or "A (——) walks into a bar . . ." jokes—but it's also fun if it's a more intimate trick. (Maybe the special someone in your life is *very* lucky?) Whatever your superpower, use your innate Spidey-sense to discover it, embrace it, and exercise it regularly.

Go to a movie alone.

You've probably always thought of going to the movies as a romantic, couple-y, Saturday-night thing to do. When you think about it, though, it doesn't have to be this way. Movies *can* be a group experience (I saw *Bridget Jones's Diary* with about a dozen women, and it was a hoot), but they can also be a decadent way to spend an afternoon alone. They don't require talking to another person (in fact, it's better if no one is yammering in your ear), and you don't have to make plans ahead of time—you can just duck into a multiplex on the spur of the moment. The best part is that you can sit wherever you want, have popcorn and Milk Duds all to yourself, and if you don't like the movie, you can get up and leave without discussion. On your way out, duck into another theater and see if you like that film better. Just be sneaky and avoid the ushers.

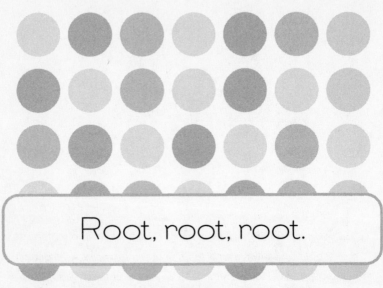

Root, root, root.

I am one of those people (okay, women) who only really start paying attention to a professional sports season once it comes down to the wire, at which point I have been known to become obsessed, especially if a local team or player is involved. I like the finality of a title-deciding triumph; if you get the chance, go to the Super Bowl or the Westminster Kennel Club Dog Show, where a true champion is crowned. As a spectator, there's nothing like witnessing the thrill of victory late in the game, especially when an underdog or an unthinkable comeback is involved. But even if it's a spelling bee, a Scrabble championship, or the local Little League game, be an active spectator. Pick a favorite team and do some loud, supportive rooting (GOOOOOAALLLLLLL!). Enjoy the moment, and rejoice with the champions while they are at the top of their game. My waterworks start up whenever I see competitors jumping with glee, dumping Gatorade, etc. Maybe it's because I know I'll never feel that particular sense of Olympic accomplishment, or perhaps I'm just sappy enough to think about their parents and how proud they must be. Then again, I also tear up at every single curtain call I see in the theater. Yes, I'm the sentimental sort.

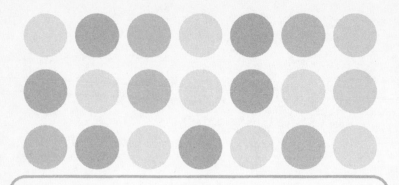

Instead of a stage name,
pick a "stage age."

L ying about my age never occurred to me until a few years ago, when I noticed my friends starting to do it, online or in person. Up until then, I'd always been proud of my age, because it means I've lived X number of years of life, surviving and growing all the while. I still am proud, but I also realize that little white lies never hurt anyone, especially if they give you a little rush, or an edge. Consider your audience when you lie—if you're at a twentysomething party and feeling out of place, well, when in Rome . . . Just don't be one of those women who, when asked her age, says coyly, "How old do you *think* I am?" That's just annoying: it puts people on the spot, and it might backfire—you're in for a rude awakening if you don't get the answer you're hoping for.

Lose gracefully.

As a child, it was acceptable (mildly) to be a sore loser: the pouting, the stormy glares, the whining. As an adult, none of that is even remotely appealing, though we all know it still happens regularly. (Off the top of your head, I know you can think of one coworker who fits this bill.) As you mature, be conscious of your attitude toward competition: whether it's losing out on a promotion at work, on a guy whose affection you think you want, or on the lead in the local play, you don't have to send flowers to your opponent, but you should learn to take the high road. Congratulate the person who bested you and sincerely wish her well; this will make you the bigger person, and it will earn you enormous respect as a worthy opponent. If you are sincere in your congratulations, you will be better off inside, too—being a sore loser is not a healthy way to live. After the agony passes, you can continue to reassess your loss, work on improving your skills, and vow to win the next round. On the bright side, loss builds character, and how you bounce back defines you as a person. Losing is not always as bad as we fear it will be. And if we were always on the winning team, victory would lose some of its sweetness.

Surprise someone.

What's more fun than throwing a big bash and inviting everyone you know? The fact that the guest of honor has no idea what's coming. Being devious is something most of us don't get to do very often, and it's even more rare to be thanked once we're discovered. Pick an occasion—your parents' anniversary, your best buddy's engagement, your sister's baby shower—recruit some comrades-in-arms, and start planning. (Just make sure the guest of honor is stout of heart and fond of surprises: even if you're lucky enough to have a ninety-year-old grandfather, do you really want to risk surprising him at that age?) Consider a theme around which gifts can center, but make it classy, not cheesy—for my cousin Kelly's fortieth birthday, we all bought special bottles of wine and gave her an instant wine cellar. Develop your guest list, and make sure everyone is in the know; keeping the secret can be as much fun as the party itself. Fly people in from out of town and keep them hidden until the reveal. Hit upon a great way to get the guest of honor there without raising suspicion. Make it a night to remember.

Ride in a limo.

You may have met this goal on prom night in 1986, but does it really count if you fit twenty people into the back of the smallest stretch possible? I think not. This time, be a little more extravagant. Pick a romantic occasion and invite a special someone to join you for an excursion to remember. Go wine-tasting in the country, have dinner and see a sold-out show, or just drive around and take in the sights. No one has to be the designated driver, and I guarantee you will feel like a rock star (strangers will wonder who's inside), even without a red carpet at your destination. In fact, the destination doesn't even matter—take advantage of the tinted-window privacy, and make your own magic in the backseat. You may not have done that since 1986, either.

Hang up your
binoculars.

My first arena concert ever was in 1980: Barry Manilow, in all his Copacabana glory (thanks, Dad!). Even now, I can still taste the anticipation I felt in the preceding weeks. Since then, my tastes have changed, in both genre and venue. Live music can be inspiring, but it's so much better in smaller halls (and when you know the artist's catalogue well). I've seen a lot of concerts in my day, and in general, I know that I've outgrown arena shows—tickets are outrageous, the bands look like ants from where I sit, and there are usually puking teenagers surrounding me. Check your local listings and pick one band to be your last hurrah. Get the best seats you can, scream your lungs out, and then make that long trek to the parking lot for the last time. One caveat: Bruce Springsteen will always be my exception. No matter where he plays, The Boss rocks and so does the E Street Band. So my advice to you is twofold: Vow never to go to an arena concert again, but break your vow the minute Bruce and the boys get back together. You won't regret it.

Let the spirit move you.

Religious beliefs and their lifestyle manifestations are very personal choices, and obviously best left to the individual. Maybe you grew up going to church and Sunday school every week. Once you got to college, Sundays became a time of catching up with friends, doing homework, and generally recuperating from the weekend. These days, your Sunday service is typically *Meet the Press* (will that give Tim Russert a god complex?). If you feel like something is missing in your life, start slow—visit a local temple, mosque, or church. Don't let a religion-free youth hold you back; exploration is healthy, and you don't have to blindly follow in your family's footsteps. Religious communities are always welcoming and can be quite socially active. At the very least, services can give you a quiet hour or two—with no phone, no TV (sorry, Tim), and no chaos—to reorder your thoughts each week. Or, yoga might be your way of connecting to something spiritual deep inside you. Create your own oasis at home through meditation. Take a deep breath and enjoy.

Sleep under the stars.

You may think camping is something that sounds more fun than it is, but actually I think it's the other way around. What sounds fun about peeing outside and counting the insects invading your space? The truth is, in our ever-changing world, twenty-four hours without any technology to speak of is an incomparable gift to yourself. If you live in a big city, the stars are usually diluted by the bright lights, and when do you look up at the sky, anyway? Remedy this situation. Pick a weekend with a full moon, grab a few buddies (make sure at least one of you has a guitar) and your sleeping bag, and head for the hills. Bring plenty of hot dogs and fixins for s'mores, and pick a spot with a full view of the heavens above. Sing songs of your childhood around the campfire, toast those marshmallows to a crisp, and fall asleep basking in the glow of Mother Nature's warm blanket of stars. The next morning, brush the leaves (and bugs) from your hair, find a big tree to pee behind, and take a hike.

Give something back.

I feel quite lucky to be where I am in life: with a good job, a place to live, and friends and family who support me, I feel fairly certain I can do anything. When I think about all the people who are not so lucky, it sometimes overwhelms me and I have to lie down. One way to counter this ennui is to stop talking about making someone else's life better and actually DO something charitable. Make this the year that you commit yourself to improving the world. If you don't have a lot of money to spare, don't let that hold you back. Become a Big Sister, run a 10K for breast cancer research, serve Thanksgiving dinner at a shelter, or spend your Saturdays shopping for an elderly shut-in. If your job is flexible, spend one morning a week tutoring at-risk kids. If you're a financial whiz, help people set up a savings account or finish their taxes. If you *are* lucky enough to have extra capital lying around, consider potential recipients for your altruism: Pick a charity with low overhead costs and make a substantial donation. But remember, charity vaunteth not itself; the warm glow you'll feel is its own reward.

Habla sie Français?

It's been said before, but it bears repeating: Americans are seriously language-ignorant. We arrogantly expect the world to speak English to us, and they mostly, resignedly, comply. (Though who knows what they toss into our food or mutter under their breath? It's probably not complimentary.) The next time you travel abroad, defy the ugly American stereotype and plan ahead. Read up on the culture, and know what each city is famous for. Most important, learn twenty key phrases, or at least have them at your fingertips. Be creative. Know how to say the important things, like "Another bottle of wine, please," "How much does that cost?" and "Are you married?" Be able to count to twenty, and be familiar with higher numbers in case you are quoted prices. Of course, also know how to ask for the bathroom and how to hail a taxi. Even if they answer you in their native tongue and you look at them blankly, smile and shrug. They will be impressed you at least took the initiative, and you will know you've done your part for world peace.

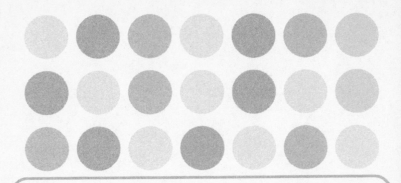

Throw out any T-shirts
with logos on them.

When I first suggested this goal, I was met with serious resistance from several friends. They feel tied to their sorority socials, their 10K evidence, and their "My parents went to Croatia, and all I got . . ." souvenirs. But T-shirts have a shelf life, especially the ones you wear. My sister had a brilliant idea—for her boyfriend's birthday, she went into his closet and collected all the pitted shirts that drove her crazy and she cut them up (risky, I know!) and turned them into a quilt in a crafts class she was taking. We're not all Martha Stewart, but we all have a creative crafter somewhere deep inside. Maybe you can take Polaroids of your favorite logos and put them all in a T-shirt scrapbook. Perhaps you can just cut out the logos themselves and make a pillowcase. Bottom line, keep five of your favorite (and newest) for your workouts, and dump the rest. Think of all the storage space you'll save. Just do it.

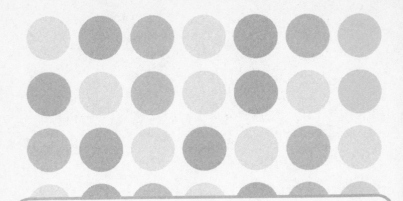

Ride a roller coaster.

The amusement parks and county fairs of my youth are a vivid blur of lines and screams and flailing arms. Immediately upon finishing the log flume, my sister and I would make a break for the runaway train, leaving the haunted house for after lunch. Those days were full of blazing sun, cotton candy, and strong stomachs, none of which I am on speaking terms with anymore. Next summer, though, channel your inner daredevil and seek out a roller coaster, preferably one that's old and rickety (à la the Cyclone at Coney Island)—but a more modern loop-de-loop will also do the trick—and take it for a spin. Wave your hands in the air like you don't care, let yourself be tossed around like a rag doll, and scream until your voice is gone. Do it before back spasms are a regular occurrence.

Have a male friend.

Women are, of course, each other's best friends. We know what it's like to find the perfect bra, we cry at commercials, and we adapt to each other's cycles. Men, however, can be terrific friends, too, if you search carefully. Yes, I'm talking about *real* friends, the kind Harry told Sally they could never be. I think to a point, Harry's right—platonic male/female relationships commonly get complicated, but I don't believe this is a rule without exception. I have several long-term friendships with men that have never crossed that non-platonic line. (And they aren't all gay.) No, they aren't my *best* friends, but they are honest, insightful, and complimentary, and the perfect beer-drinking comrades. They indulge my ignorance at football games, and even teach me the rules without patronizing. And man-oh-man, can they gossip—don't let them tell you any different.

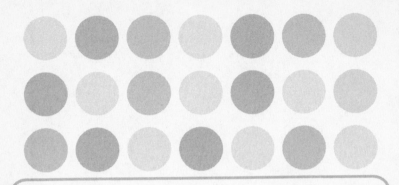

Ditch your college furniture.

You probably don't have any milk crates anymore, but do you still have that one dresser you bought at a yard sale to go in that crappy place you rented junior year? I know you like it; I know it still "works," but don't you want to have things that actually match in your bedroom? IKEA is great for filling utilitarian needs on the cheap, but there's also a lot to be said for accenting wisely: carefully select eye-catching pieces of "real" furniture that you don't have to assemble yourself. If you don't have a lot of capital, start small. Pick a room and start from scratch or build the décor around a piece you really love. Shop around. Look for a store that matches your style and attitude. Don't limit yourself to chain warehouses that cater to the lowest common denominator.

Name something.

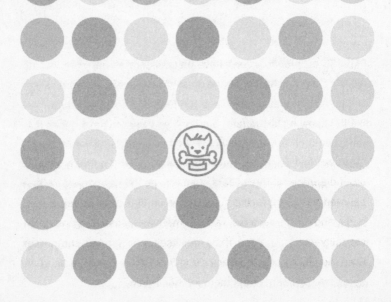

I've always been obsessed with names, poring over baby name books with pregnant friends or scanning the marina for clever boat monikers. Unless you're Sean Combs, names are usually permanent. A name gives something (someone!) character, personality, and often, goals to live up to. A few years ago, I was delighted when my friend Ellen took my suggestion for her daughter's name: she had parameters and I took them seriously. I feel bonded with this child (not that I wouldn't have otherwise), and secretly proud. Anything can have a name, really—a house, a car (my family traveled around Europe for three years in an orange VW van named Betsy—I believed her black racing stripes gave us that extra edge), a computer, and of course, a pet. Make something permanent; ensure immortality—for the person/thing/pet itself, and for you, the namer. Even though my cousin Danny's dog Bob Barker met a sad and untimely end, his name (and memory) will live on.

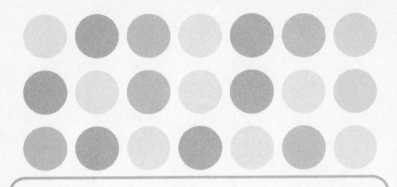

Divorce your hairstylist,
or at least cheat.

When you look at photos of yourself from ten years ago, do you notice that your cut is exactly the same length, give or take an inch? We all fall into this trap when we go to the same hairstylist for a decade. It's easy to do—we get into a rut, we become comfortable with the same person, the prices don't go up much for loyal customers . . . but sometimes enough is enough. Styles change, but hairdressers can stick with cuts they've given since their beauty school days. Break free. Make an appointment at a new, hip salon. Spend a little more—you are worth it. You might feel guilty of desertion, but a pair of fresh eyes can do wonders. I once had a hairdresser tell me that no one over thirty should have bangs (which I'd had for twenty years), and he convinced me to grow mine out; I appreciated it at the time, but I've since divorced him. Good thing, because bangs are back. I wonder if he knows.

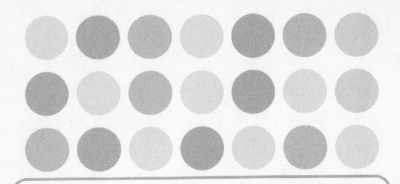

Get someone else to
love your favorite movie.

There's nothing special about loving *The Godfather,* but it takes a lot to admit to loving something others think is rubbish, and it takes even more to convince them to see the light. To that end, here we go: I love, love, *love Joe vs. the Volcano,* perhaps one of the worst-reviewed movies of all time. It gives me a lump in my throat just thinking about it. And I can quote it line for line. The thing is, my friend Stephanie was the one who convinced me of its genius. And now, once in a blue moon, I serendipitously meet one of those very special people who can read the same magical optimism in between the lines of the silliness. I LOVE these people. That's the easy part, though—it's much more difficult to try to change someone's mind. Don't try too hard or build it up so much that no reality can match expectations. Instead, move in slow. Have your evidence ready; you need to be able to articulate *why* you love this particular movie so much. You might have to trick your friend into watching it, or use reverse psychology. By the way, have you seen it?

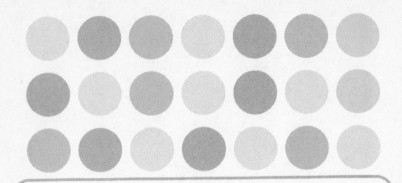

Take the long
way home.

So often, we yearn to get away, to explore new worlds and experience different ways of life. But how well do you know your own town? Next time you want a weekend getaway, but have neither the time nor the money to get extravagant, explore your options right around the corner. See your town the way others see it, from a whole new perspective. Start by driving home a different way; you may discover charming side streets you've never noticed before. Even if it doesn't save you time, it just might be a prettier drive. If you live in a big city, visit a tourist attraction you've always avoided (preferably in the off-season), and revel in your tourist-ness. If your town does not have a zillion options, ask your friends about their favorite things to do—you may discover a new hiking trail or a hole-in-the-wall bôite to add to your regular repertoire. For a mini-getaway without airfare, splurge on a night in the fanciest hotel or inn you can find; luxuriate in the hot tub and order room service. Most of all, appreciate where you live. Bask in the knowledge that you are here year-round; while you can enjoy it anytime, others have to pay to visit.

Learn to tango.

Swaying giddily to "Stairway to Heaven" was a piece of cake at the eighth-grade dance; you had bigger things to worry about (the inevitable interlocking braces, your dad waiting in the car outside) than the proper dance steps. Things have changed a bit—are you now terrified your two left feet will betray you if you accept that invitation to dance? Well, swallow your pride and admit you don't know how to do everything, but recognize that you can *learn* to do anything. Even Ginger Rogers had to start somewhere. Sign yourself and your very own Patrick Swayze up for tango lessons (or swing, if that's more your style). Tell him you might step on his toes at first, and forgive him in advance for doing the same to you. Learn the steps in comfortable shoes, and don't worry if you have to keep an eye on your feet. With practice, you'll be able to sashay in smokin' high heels and look deep into his eyes with both confidence and a rose in your teeth. When you're ready, take your solid-gold steps and your best red dress to that club downtown, and trip the lights fantastic. This time, your dad won't be waiting up.

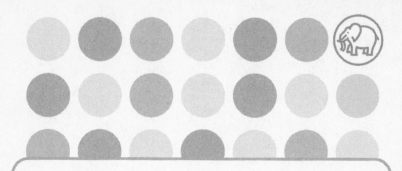

Go somewhere that makes people scratch their heads.

Most of us, when we think about vacation, dream of a week by the seashore or ten days in the Italian hills. Next time you are planning a trip, though, think outside the box. Be that person who goes someplace most people have never considered. You don't have to join the Peace Corps, but why not visit a developing country? Once you get there, travel (and massages, or sherpas!) will probably be cheap, but accommodations may be less than four-star, so steel yourself. In the past few years, my friend Jenny has been to Mongolia, Nepal, and Greenland. Can you say that about anyone you know? Sure, we scratched our heads at first, but her travelogue slideshows have been like mini-vacations for the rest of us, and have made globalization a bit less abstract.

Charm your way into
(or out of) something.

Feminine wiles are a magical thing, and they have been the subject of literature since the dawn of recorded time. Using one's charms to one's advantage goes in and out of vogue, and many of us consider ourselves too feminist to exploit them to the fullest extent. While I abhor seeing women use sex in demeaning and crass ways to get ahead, I think there are other times when you've got to be pragmatic, think on your feet, and use whatever works. Now, most of us spend the bulk of our lives in the daily equivalent of coach class. It's fine, but it's not exactly extravagant. Around you, others are getting things for nothing just by being enchanting, to men and women alike. The next time the guy behind the airport check-in counter has a flirtatious glint in his eye, exercise your charm muscle; challenge yourself to maneuver your way into his good graces and into first class. If that doesn't work, try killing the (female) check-in agent with flattering kindness; she might remember you when she needs to bump someone up to make room in coach. If you are not successful the first time, don't give up. Practice thinking on your feet and disarming others; it's a lifelong skill that will win friends and influence people. Talk your way out of a speeding ticket without resorting to tears. Convince the cable guy to give you extra channels at a discount, even for one month. Start small. Soon your boss will think of you when she has a special assignment next time. And maybe, just maybe, you'll get to experience warm chocolate-chip cookies at 30,000 feet.

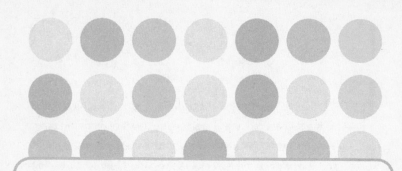

Figure out what you
want to be when
you grow up.

Some people are fortunate enough to know from childhood what career they want. Then there are the rest of us. Very rarely do life paths pan out exactly as planned: childhood interests melt into satisfying hobbies, or liberal arts majors become launching pads for careers that were never intended. And sometimes we just change our minds. So, assess your situation. Has what once challenged you now made you dread getting up in the morning? Have you begun to envision yourself in a whole new role? Luckily, gone are the days where a decision made at twenty-two has to be final. In roughly four decades of full-time work, we may career through multiple careers. If you are looking for a change, don't be deterred by inertia. Explore by talking to people in that new field, and ask detailed questions. Perhaps volunteering can be a way to ease your way in before making the official leap. If you need to go back to school, schedule an appointment with an admissions counselor, and start saving up for tuition. (You won't be the oldest one there; I know a woman who went to medical school in her fifties.) If you are daunted by the thought of starting over, weigh that fear against your current day-to-day drudgery. Maybe staying where you are is the right move after all; with a renewed sense of purpose, you can win that promotion you've been ambivalent about. A career doesn't have to complete you, but it should give you relative satisfaction.

Colorize.

ook around you. What is the brightest color you see? If it's the red *K* on your cereal box, you've got some work to do. As adults, many of us go through life blending in and not making any waves. We easily fall into the trap of neutrality—by not calling attention to ourselves, we can fly under the radar in an unassuming fashion. Well, where's the excitement in that? Take a look at your wardrobe—are you addicted to black, beige, and white because they always go together? Life should not always be so mix-and-match. Next time you're shopping, let yourself get carried away by a hot-pink raincoat—what better way to cheer you up in a thunderstorm? You don't have to go overboard, but a little color here and there makes your blood race and your cheeks blush. A style palette can attract attention in a good way. I'm not advocating blue eye shadow by any means, but how about initiating a scavenger hunt for the perfect red lipstick that will draw attention to your sparkling smile, and to the ideas coming out of your mouth? Make a statement with a signature green handbag; next season, pick another color. When you set the table, offset your white dishes with orange placemats. Maybe you have a deep-seated affinity for crisp white linens, but you can paint your bedroom turquoise, or magenta, or eggplant. Start with one wall . . .

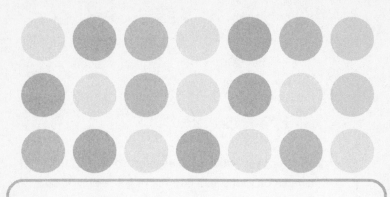

Never show up
empty-handed.

N ow that you know how to host a great dinner party, turn the tables a bit and think about what kind of guest you want to be. One way of endearing yourself to others (and proving your innate good manners) is to always bring something to the table. Whether it's a birthday celebration or a casual cocktail party, think ahead and come up with a personalized hostess gift. Flowers may not be so unique, but if you remember that your hosts just got back from a trip to Amsterdam, pick out tulips for the occasion. If you are spending the weekend with friends who have children, bring a kid-friendly video along, or a copy of *Free to Be You and Me*. Sometimes the most banal of gifts can be livened up with creative presentation: Instead of wrapping paper, use colorful tinfoil or subway maps. If your friend knits, replace the bow with a skein of yarn. Your special effort will be appreciated, and going that extra mile allows you to make a great impression, especially when you're meeting someone (his parents?) for the first time.

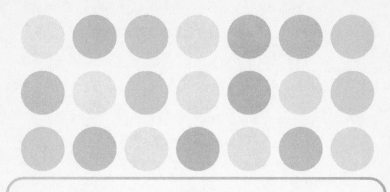

Bring something
back to life.

It's often said that one man's trash is another man's treasure. While I would stop short of Dumpster-diving, the ability to see the potential in something discarded by someone else demonstrates a very resourceful nature. Yard-saling is big business in some places—my friend Tanessa and her husband treat it like a Saturday morning sport, and have furnished their house beautifully with hidden treasures previously cast aside. A little paint and refinishing can resurrect almost anything, injecting it with a renewed sense of purpose. Speaking of resurrection, if someone at work is giving up on a ficus tree, consider the possibility that his or her thumb just isn't as green as yours. And while dogs abandoned at the shelter aren't exactly dead (yet), they need a new lease on life. If you have the room, and the patience, why not adopt one? In most cases, with love and tenderness, you can develop one of the most meaningful (and mutually beneficial) relationships of your life. All these examples share the common denominator of looking beyond the surface. Use your own unique vision to expand the possibilities, and bring something back to life.

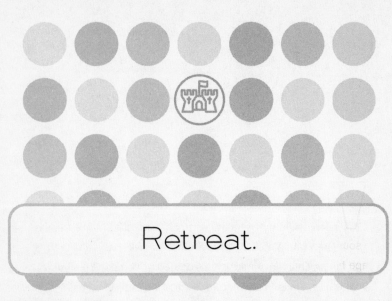

Retreat.

Where do you go when you need to be alone? When you need to escape the chaos of cell phones, screaming children, e-mail, traffic, your mile-long To-Do list? Not to sound like a Calgon commercial, but it's important to have an escape hatch when the pressure reaches the boiling point. Your personal retreat might be your Jacuzzi tub, with a bath pillow, candles, and soothing music. Or it might be a special room in your house that is completely *yours,* no guests allowed. If you aren't fortunate enough to have a whole room to yourself, pick a corner and decorate it lushly, with a comfortable chair, a footrest, and a good reading light. If your house is the last place you can relax—thanks to all those other people who share your life—find a secret getaway. My friend Katie loves the public library, with its cavernous ceilings and quiet hush. The gym is another good place where your mind can wander while you work out tension, kinks, and excess energy. Amy swears by her weekly manicure/pedicure, which she gets while sitting in an electric massage chair. Your retreat might just be portable—plug in your iPod, turn it up loud, and escape into oblivion no matter where you are (but promise me you won't do this while driving). Once you've rejuvenated, life will once again be manageable.

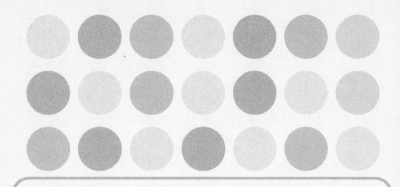

Accept that forty is
the new thirty.

So you're turning forty, and you're whining about it. Boo hoo. Get over yourself. Life is full of ups and downs and ins and outs, and you don't get to pack it in until the very end. I used to scoff at people in their fifties who said, "But I still feel twenty-two!" Now, however, I know exactly what they mean. And isn't that great? I'd rather feel twenty-two than fifty-five. Middle age does not mean what it used to. Age is a only a state of mind—cliché, but true. I know vibrant, electric souls who are considered elderly, and I have seen teenagers who are ancient beyond their years. Look to the future with anticipation and wonder. Think of how many changes the world has seen since you were born. Then think of all that's still to come. Find activities that will sustain you and keep you young (yoga, swimming, and gardening come to mind), and surround yourself with people who love you. The world will be your oyster for decades to come. Lighten up, consider your forties a clean slate, and enjoy!